A LITTLE BOOK OF

Love Poems

With fine art illustrations

To: _____

From: _____

Contents

A Little Book of

Love Poems

UPON JULIA'S CLOTHES

WHENAS IN SILKS my Julia goes,
Why then, methinks, how sweetly flows
The liquefaction of her clothes!

Next, when I cast mine eyes and see
That vibration each way free,
-O how that glittering taketh me!

ROBERT HERRICK
(1591-1674)

APPLETREE PRESS

from EPITHALAMION

Tell me, ye merchants' daughters, did ye see
So fayre a creature in your town before;
So sweet, so lovely and so mild as she,
Adorned with beautyes grace and vertues store?
Her goodly eyes like Saphyres shining bright,
Her forehead yvory white?
Her cheeks like apples which the sun hath rudded,
Her lips like cherryes charming men to byte,
Her breast like to a bowl of creame uncrudded,
Her paps like lyllies budded,
Her snowy neck like to a marble towre;
And all her body like a pallace fayre,
Ascending up, with many a stately stayre,
To honor's seat and chastitys sweet bowre.
Why stand ye still ye virgins in amaze,
Upon her so to gaze
While ye forget your former lay to sing,
To which the woods did answer, and your echo ring?

Edmund Spenser
(1552–1599)

CARDS AND KISSES

Cupid and my Campaspe play'd
At cards for kisses – Cupid paid:
He stakes his quiver, bows and arrows,
His mother's doves, and teams of sparrows;
Loses them too: then down he throws
The coral of his lips, the rose
Growing on's cheek (but none knows how);
With these, the crystal of his brow,
And then the dimple of his chin:
All these did my Campaspe win.
At last he set her both his eyes –
She won, and Cupid blind did rise.
O Love! Has she done this for thee?
What shall, alas, become of me?

John Lyly
(1554–1606)

8

The Bargain

My true love hath my heart, and I have his,
By just exchange one for the other given:
I hold his dear, and mine he cannot miss,
There never was a better bargain driven:
My true love hath my heart, and I have his.

His heart in me keeps him and me in one,
My heart in him his thoughts and senses guides:
He loves my heart, for once it was his own,
I cherish his because in me it bides:
My true love hath my heart, and I have his.

Sir Philip Sidney
(1554–1586)

THE PASSIONATE SHEPHERD TO HIS LOVE

Come live with me and be my love,
And we will all the pleasures prove
That hills, valleys, dales and fields,
Or woods or steepy mountains yields.

And we will sit upon the rocks,
And see the shepherds feed their flocks
By shallow rivers, to whose falls
Melodious birds sing madrigals.

And I will make thee beds of roses
And a thousand fragrant posies;
A cap of flowers, and a kirtle
Embroider'd all with leaves of myrtle.

A gown made of the finest wool
Which from our pretty lambs we pull;
Fair-lined slippers for the cold,
With buckles of the purest gold.

A belt of straw and ivy-buds
With coral clasps and amber-studs:
And if these pleasures may thee move,
Come live with me and be my Love.

Christopher Marlowe
(1564–1593)

It Was a Lover and His Lass

It was a lover and his lass,
With a hey, and a ho, and a hey nonino,
That o'er the green cornfield did pass,
In the spring time, the only pretty ring time,
When birds do sing, hey ding a ding, ding;
Sweet lovers love the spring.

Between the acres of the rye,
With a hey, and a ho, and a hey nonino,
These pretty country folks would lie,
In the spring time, the only pretty ring time,
When birds do sing, hey ding a ding, ding;
Sweet lovers love the spring.

This carol they began that hour,
With a hey, and a ho, and a hey nonino,
How that life was but a flower
In the spring time, the only pretty ring time,
When birds do sing, hey ding a ding, ding;
Sweet lovers love the spring.

And, therefore, take the present time,
With a hey, and a ho, and a hey nonino,
for love is crowned with the prime
In the spring time, the only pretty ring time,
When birds do sing, hey ding a ding, ding;
Sweet lovers love the spring.

William Shakespeare
(1564–1616)

SONNET

When, in disgrace with Fortune and men's eyes,
I all alone beweep my outcast state,
And trouble deaf heaven with my bootless cries,
And look upon myself, and curse my fate,
Wishing me like to one more rich in hope,
Featured like him, like him with friends possest,
Desiring this man's art and that man's scope,
With what I most enjoy contented least;
Yet in these thoughts almost myself despising –
Haply I think on thee: and then my state,
Like to the lark at break of day arising
From sullen earth, sings hymns at heaven's gate;
For thy sweet love remember'd such wealth brings
That then I scorn to change my state with kings.

William Shakespeare
(1564–1616)

CHERRY RIPE

There is a garden in her face
Where roses and white lilies blow;
A heavenly paradise is that place,
Wherein all pleasant fruits do flow:
There cherries grow which none may buy
Till 'Cherry-ripe' themselves do cry.

These cherries fairly do enclose
Of orient pearls a double row,
Which when her lovely laughter shows,
They look like rosebuds filled with snow;
Yet them nor peer nor prince can buy
Till 'Cherry-ripe' themselves do cry.

Her eyes like angels watch them still;
Her brows like bended bows do stand,
Threat'ning with piercing frowns to kill
All that attempt with eye or hand
Those sacred cherries to come nigh,
Till 'Cherry-ripe' themselves do cry.

Thomas Campion
(d. 1620)

from THE GOOD MORROW

I wonder by my troth, what thou, and I,
Did, till we lov'd? were we not wean'd till then?
But suck'd on country pleasures childishly?
Or snorted we in the seven sleepers' den?
'Twas so; But this, all pleasures fancies be.
If ever any beauty I did see,
Which I desir'd, and got, 'twas but a dream of thee.

…

My face in thine eye, thine in mine appears,
And true plain hearts do in the faces rest,
Where can we find two better hemispheres
Without sharp North, without declining West?
Whatever dies, was not mixt equally;
If our two loves be one, or, thou and I
Love so alike, that none do slacken, none can die.

John Donne
(1573–1631)

TO ELECTRA

I dare not ask a kiss,
I dare not beg a smile,
Lest having that, or this,
I might grow proud the while.

No no, the utmost share
Of my desire shall be
Only to kiss that air
That lately kissed thee.

Robert Herrick
(1591–1674)

UPON JULIA'S CLOTHES

Whenas in silks my Julia goes,
Why then, methinks, how sweetly flows
The liquefaction of her clothes!

Next, when I cast mine eyes and see
That brave vibration each way free,
– O how that glittering taketh me!

Robert Herrick
(1591–1674)

WHY SO PALE AND WAN?

Why so pale and wan, fond lover?
Prithee, why so pale?
Will, when looking well can't move her,
Looking ill prevail?
Prithee, why so pale?

Why so dull and mute, young sinner?
Prithee, why so mute?
Will, when speaking well can't win her
Saying nothing do't?
Prithee, why so mute?

Quit, quit, for shame! This will not move;
This cannot take her.
If of herself she will not love,
Nothing can make her:
The devil take her!

Sir John Suckling
(1609–1642)

CHLORIS IN THE SNOW

I saw fair Chloris walk alone,
When feather'd rain came softly down,
As Jove descending from his Tower
To court her in a silver shower:

The wanton snow flew to her breast,
Like pretty birds into their nest,
But, overcome with whiteness there,
For grief it thaw'd into a tear:
Thence falling on her garments' hem,
To deck her, froze into a gem.

William Strode
(1602–1645)

Hidden Flame

I feed a flame within, which so torments me
That it both pains my heart, and yet contents me:
'Tis such a pleasing smart, and I so love it,
That I had rather die than once remove it.

Yet he, for whom I grieve, shall never know it;
My tongue does not betray, nor my eyes show it.
Not a sigh, nor a tear, my pain discloses,
But they fall silently, like dew on roses.

Thus, to prevent my Love from being cruel,
My heart's the sacrifice, as 'tis the fuel;
And while I suffer this to give him quiet,
My faith rewards my love, though he deny it.

On his eyes will I gaze, and there delight me;
While I conceal my love no frown can fright me.
To be more happy I dare not aspire,
Nor can I fall more low, mounting no higher.

John Dryden
(1631–1700)

JOHN ANDERSON, MY JO

John Anderson, my jo, John,
When we were first acquent,
Your locks were like the raven,
Your bonny brow was brent;
But now your brow is beld, John,
Your locks are like the snaw.
But blessings on your frosty pow,
John Anderson, my jo.

John Anderson, my jo, John,
We clamb the hill the gither
And many a canty day, John,
We've had wi' ane anither:
Now we maun totter down, John,
And hand in hand we'll go,
And sleep the gither at the foot,
John Anderson, my jo.

Robert Burns
(1759–1796)

A WISH

Mine be a cot beside the hill:
A bee-hive's hum shall soothe my ear;
A willowy brook, that turns a mill,
With many a fall shall linger near.

The swallow oft beneath my thatch
Shall twitter from his clay-built nest;
Oft shall the pilgrim lift the latch
And share my meal, a welcome guest.

Around my ivied porch shall spring
Each fragrant flower that drinks the dew;
And Lucy at her wheel shall sing
In russet gown and apron blue.

The village church among the trees,
Where first our marriage vows were given,
With merry peals shall swell the breeze,
And point with taper spire to heaven.

Samuel Rogers
(1763–1855)

LUCY

She dwelt among the untrodden ways
Beside the springs of Dove,
A maid whom there were none to praise
And very few to love.

A violet by a mossy stone
Half-hidden from the eye!
– Fair as a star, when only one
Is shining in the sky.

She lived unknown, and few could know,
When Lucy ceased to be;
But she is in her grave, and, oh,
The difference to me!

William Wordsworth
(1770–1850)

WE'LL GO NO MORE A-ROVING

So, we'll go no more a-roving
So late into the night,
Though the heart be still as loving
And the moon be still as bright.

For the sword outwears its sheath,
And the soul wears out the breast,
And the heart must pause to breathe,
And love itself must rest.

Though the night was made for loving,
And the day returns too soon,
Yet we'll go no more a-roving
By the light of the moon.

George Gordon Noel, Lord Byron
(1788–1824)

SAY, WHAT IS LOVE

Say, what is love? To live in vain,
To love, and die, and love again?
Say, what is love? Is it to be
In prison still and still be free –
Or seem as free? Alone, and prove
The hopeless hopes of real love?
Does real love on earth exist?
'Tis like a sunbeam in the mist,
That fades and nowhere wil remain,
And nowhere is o'ertook again.
Say, what is love? A blooming name,
A rose-leaf on the page of fame,
That blows, then fades, to cheat no more,
And is what nothing was before?
Say, what is love? Whate'er it be
It centres, Mary, still with thee.

John Clare
(1793–1864)

LAST SONNET

Bright Star! Would I were steadfast as thou art –
Not in lone splendour hung aloft the night,
And watching, with eternal lids apart,
Like Nature's patient sleepless Eremite,
The moving waters at their priest-like task
Of pure ablution round earth's human shores
Or gazing on the new soft-fallen mask
Of snow upon the mountains and the moors –
No – yet still steadfast, still unchangeable,
Pillow'd upon my fair love's ripening breast,
To feel for ever its soft rise and swell,
Awake for ever in a sweet unrest,
Still, still to hear her tender-taken breath,
And so live ever – or else swoon to death.

John Keats
(1795–1821)

Sonnet IV *from*
Sonnets from the Portuguese

If thou must love me, let it be for naught
Except for love's sake only. Do not say,
'I love her for her smile – her look – her way
Of speaking gently, – for a trick of thought
That falls in well with mine, and certes brought
A sense of pleasant ease on such a day' –
For these things in themselves, Beloved, may
Be changed, or change for thee – and love so
    wrought,
May be unwrought so. Neither love me for
Thine own dear pity's wiping my cheeks dry:
A creature might forget to weep, who bore
Thy comfort long, and lose thy love thereby!
But love me for love's sake, that evermore
Thou may'st love on, through love's eternity.

Elizabeth Barrett Browning
(1806–1861)

I Do Not Love Thee

I do not love thee! – no! I do not love thee!
And yet when thou art absent I am sad;
And envy even the bright blue sky above thee,
Whose quiet stars may see thee and be glad.

I do not love thee! – yet, I know not why,
Whate'er thou dost seems still well done, to me:
And often in my solitude I sigh
That those I do love are not more like thee!

I do not love thee! – yet, when thou art gone,
I hate the sound (though those who speak be dear)
Which breaks the lingering echo of the tone
Thy voice of music leaves upon my ear.

I do not love thee! – yet thy speaking eyes,
With their deep, bright and most expressive blue,
Between me and the midnight heavens arise,
Oftener than any eyes I ever knew.

I know I do not love thee! – yet, alas,
Others will scarcely trust my candid heart;
And oft I catch them smiling as they pass,
Because they see me gazing where thou art.

Caroline Elizabeth Sarah Norton
(1808–1877)

THE MILLER'S DAUGHTER

It is the miller's daughter,
And she has grown so dear, so dear,
That I would be the jewel
That trembles in her ear:
For hid in ringlets day and night,
I'd touch her neck so warm and white.

And I would be the girdle,
About her dainty dainty waist,
And her heart would beat against me,
In sorrow and in rest:
And I should know if it beat right,
I'd clasp it round so close and tight.

And I would be the necklace,
And all day long to fall and rise
Upon her balmy bosom,
With her laughter or her sighs:
And I would lie so light, so light,
I scarce should be unclasp'd at night.

Alfred, Lord Tennyson
(1809–1892)

47

In a Gondola

The moth's kiss, first!
Kiss me as if you made me believe
You were not sure, this eve,
How my face, your flower, had pursed
Its petals up; so, here and there
You brush it, till I grow aware
Who wants me, and wide ope I burst.

The bee's kiss, now!
Kiss me as if you enter'd gay
My heart at some noonday,
A bud that dares not disallow
The claim, so all is render'd up,
And passively its shattered cup
Over your head to sleep I bow.

Robert Browning
(1812–1889)

THE APPEAL

If grief for grief can touch thee,
If answering woe for woe,
If any ruth can melt thee,
Come to me now!

I cannot be more lonely,
More drear I cannot be!
My worn heart throbs so wildly,
'Twill break for thee.

And when the world despises,
When Heaven repels my prayer,
Will not mine angel comfort?
Mine idol hear?

Yes, by the tears I've poured thee,
By all my hours of pain,
Oh, I shall surely win thee,
Beloved, again!

Emily Brontë
(1818–1848)

from LOVE IN THE VALLEY

Under yonder beech-tree single on the green-sward,
Couch'd with her arms behind her golden head,
Knees and tresses folded to slip and ripple idly,
Lies my young love sleeping in the shade.
Had I the heart to slide an arm beneath her,
Press her parting lips as her waist I gather slow,
Waking in amazement she could not but embrace me:
Then would she hold me and never let me go?

Shy as the squirrel and wayward as the swallow,
Swift as the swallow along the river's light
Circleting the surface to meet his mirror'd winglets,
Fleeter she seems in her stay than in her flight.
Shy as the squirrel that leaps among the pine-tops,
Wayward as the swallow overhead at set of sun,
She whom I love is hard to catch and conquer,
Hard, but O the glory of the winning were she won!

When her mother tends her before the laughing mirror,
Tying up her laces, looping up her hair,
Often she thinks, were this wild thing wedded,
More love should I have, and much less care.
When her mother tends her before the lighted mirror,
Loosening her laces, combing down her curls,
Often she thinks, were this wild thing wedded,
I should miss but one for many boys and girls.

George Meredith
(1828–1909)

52

The Voice

Woman much missed, how you call to me, call
   to me,
Saying that now you are not as you were
When you had changed from the one who was
   all to me,
But as at first, when our day was fair.

Can it be you that I hear? Let me view you, then,
Standing as when I drew near to the town
Where you would wait for me: yes, as I knew
   you then,
Even to the original air-blue gown!

Or is it only the breeze, in its listlessness
Travelling across the wet meads to me here,
You being ever dissolved in wan wistlessness,
Heard no more again far or near?

Thus I: faltering forward,
Leaves around me falling,
Wind oozing thin through the thorn from norward,
And the woman calling.

Thomas Hardy
(1840–1928)

THE LADY OF THE LAMBS

She walks – the lady of my delight –
A shepherdess of sheep.
Her flocks are thoughts. She keeps them white;
She guards them from the steep.
She feeds them on the fragrant height,
And folds them in for sleep.

She roams maternal hills and bright,
Dark valleys safe and deep.
Her dreams are innocent at night;
The chastest stars may peep.
She walks – the lady of my delight –
A shepherdess of sheep.

She holds her little thoughts in sight,
Though gay they run and leap.
She is so circumspect and right;
She has her soul to keep.
She walks - the lady of my delight –
A shepherdess of sheep.

Alice Meynell
(1847–1922)

LOVE ON THE MOUNTAIN

My love comes down from the mountain
Through the mists of dawn;
I look, and the star of the morning
From the sky is gone.

My love comes down from the mountain
At dawn, dewy-sweet;
Did you step from the star to the mountain,
O little white feet?

O whence came your twining tresses
And your shining eyes,
But out of the gold of the morning
And the blue of the skies?

The misty mountain is burning
In the sun's red fire
And the heart in my breast is burning
And lost in desire.

I follow you into the valley,
But no word can I say;
To the East or the West I will follow
Till the dusk of my day.

Thomas Boyd
(1867–1927)

First published in 1993 by
The Appletree Press Ltd,
19-21 Alfred Street,
Belfast BT2 8DL
Tel: +44 232 243 074 Fax: +44 232 246 756

A Little Book of Love Poems

A catalogue record for this book is available
from the British Library.

ISBN 0-86281-454-5

9 8 7 6 5 4 3 2

Acknowledgements are due to the following
for illustrations: the National Gallery of Ireland,
Dublin and the Hugh Lane Municipal Gallery
of Modern Art, Dublin.